SWEET
PERSUASION

PAUL KARASIK

SWEET PERSUASION

The Illustrated Guide to Unparalleled Management Success

Copyright 1992 by Paul Karasik
All rights reserved. This book may not be
reproduced in whole or in part in any
manner without permission from the author,
except for brief quotations in critical
articles or reviews. Write to The
Business Institute, 899 Boulevard East,
Weehawken, NJ 07087.

Manufactured in the USA

1   2   3   4   5   6   7   8   9   10   PBK

ISBN 0-13-756255-1 PBK

ISBN 0-13-063025-X PKG

PRENTICE HALL
Career & Personal Development
Englewood Cliffs, NJ 07632
Simon & Schuster, A Paramount Communications Company

To My Parents
Nat and Leah Karasik
With Love and Gratitude

Acknowledgments

Through the years I have had the
good fortune to experience truly great
leaders, who have taught me the principles
contained in this book and have inspired
me to provide others with the tools
for success.

My family, particularly Marilyn and Fred
Portnoy, has encouraged and supported my
career and this book. Thanks also to my
friends Moss Jacobs, Saul Ellenbogen,
Lynne Lindahl, and Tanha.

A special thanks to illustrator Jo Ann
Goldsmith and my editor and dearest
friend, Gary Karasik.

Preface

If you master the art of sweet persuasion,
and learn to sell, whether it is
yourself, a product, or an idea,
your opportunity to achieve success
is unlimited.

The concepts, strategies,
and techniques contained within
can be applied to any interaction
in which you would like to influence
or motivate the actions of others.

This book is dedicated to those who
seek to master this art.

Paul Karasik

Contents

Introduction

Let's face it.
You can't do it alone.
You need the help of others
to get things done.
Now you can get that help.
Now there is Sweet Persuasion.

If your personal success depends on
achieving results through people,
if you would like to create more
productive relationships,
if you want to be recognized
as the person who gets the job done,
this could be the most important book
you will ever read.

Chapter One

What Is Sweet Persuasion?

Sweet Persuasion is inducing someone to
take action that will produce
positive results for *both of you.*

Sweet Persuasion feels good.

Successful salespeople now use Sweet Persuasion.
It helps them to achieve their sales goals.
It helps them enjoy what they are doing.
Now, successful managers
can use Sweet Persuasion too.

Sweet Persuasion feels good.

Managing is creating.
Managing is selling.
You begin with goals.
You begin with a vision.
You begin with action that needs to be taken.
You sell them to others.

You create harmonious relationships.
You create satisfaction.
You create profits.
You create a winning team.
You create quality.
You create people
who are as motivated as you.

Your management style should flow:
Rhythm, harmony, melody.

When I was a child, I asked my father,
a successful businessman,
what I needed to become a success.
Without hesitation he said,
"You've got to believe
100% in yourself,
100% in your organization, and
100% in the product of your efforts.

When you go out the door in the morning,
sell yourself,
sell your organization,
sell your ideas.

You'll never achieve greatness
unless you are 100%."

Chapter Two

What Makes People Tick?

Human nature is simple:

Most people spend the greater part
of each day thinking about themselves.
Most people want to get more
of what they want or need.

All people want more
Recognition
Money
Love
Satisfaction
Security
Health
Beauty
Peace of mind
Joy
Intimacy
Status
Success
Happiness
Etc.

If you possess the ability
to determine exactly
what people want or need
and are able to provide it,
they will give you what you want.
You will achieve your goals.
You will become a great manager.

You will achieve your goals
when your people perceive your vision and
believe in the value of your vision,
and it becomes their vision as well.

Everyone is listening
to the same radio station.

22

What's In It For Me?

Everything you do,
everything you say,
must be geared
to answering this question.

"It is one of the most
beautiful compensations of this life,
that no man can sincerely
try to help another
without helping himself."

Emerson

Take an interest in the needs of others,

and they'll take an interest in you.

It's a natural law:
You receive as much as you give.

Adopt an attitude of giving.
Give attention.
Give recognition.
Give your time.
You will feel good.

Adopt an attitude of giving.
Your success will multiply.

Altruism is selfish.

Chapter Three

How to Stay Motivated

When you need motivation, answer this:
What's in it for me if I achieve
my long- and short-term goals
and am more successful as a manager?

1. _____
2. _____
3. _____
4. _____
5. _____
6. _____
7. _____
8. _____
9. _____
10. _____

If you can't answer this question, give this
book to someone who is hungry for success.

Motivation is not a matter of will-power.
Motivation is a matter of want-power.

Take a moment.
Close your eyes.
Recall a time you achieved a major goal
or when you experienced a moment of triumph.
Recall how you felt.

This feeling is your <u>Personal Success Factor.</u>

Stay hungry for this feeling.
Stay hungry for success.
Super managers are always super hungry.

When you need motivation,
focus on this feeling.
When you are tired,
focus on this feeling.
When you are in a slump,
focus on this feeling.
When you need
to overcome the fear of rejection,
focus on this feeling.

If you focus on this feeling,
SUCCESS IS GUARANTEED.

Chapter Four

Why Johnny Can't Manage

Do you know how children learn?
The same way you do:
By example.

If you want to be a great manager,
become a great motivator.
If you want to be a great motivator,
look at a great manager
who is a great motivator.
Do exactly as that person does.
You can be a great motivator too.

If you want to become a winner,
look at a manager who is a winner.
Do exactly as this person does.
You can be a winner too.

Look around. Find a model of excellence.
When you find a great manager,
a great motivator, spend time with this person.
You will learn quickly and easily.
You will become a great manager too.

As a young man I possessed considerable
talent as a basketball player. In fact, in
my neighborhood, I was considered one of the
best players.

Up on the hill in back of the high school,
the older, more experienced
players could be found.

Although it felt good to be the local hero,
it was not until I began to play basketball
up on the hill
that my performance really improved.

Go up on the hill.
Play with those who are better than you are.
Being smart is knowing
that there are things you don't know.
And always say," Thank you."
Humility pays dividends.

38

Who is the best manager
you have ever met?

List the traits or qualities
that contribute to this person's success:

1. _____

2. _____

3. _____

4. _____

5. _____

Check the one you believe is most important.

The Anatomy of the Super Persuader

SUCCESS LEAVES CLUES.

Chapter Five

Why Johnny Can Manage

My first business experience occurred when I
was eight years old. A boy in our class
suffered from cerebral palsy. My friends
and I decided to raise funds for the United
Cerebral Palsy Association with a puppet show.

We made the puppets, wrote the script, and
then sold the tickets door-to-door. As we
would approach each door I would think to
myself, "What an adventure this is!"

Sometimes we would be invited in for milk
and cookies, and sometimes the door would
close quickly on us. We knocked on lots of
doors. We sold lots of five-cent tickets.
We raised over twenty dollars. Our
hometown paper wrote a story about us.

We were persistent, committed,
enthusiastic, and confident.

"Nothing in the world can take the place
of persistence.
Talent will not;
nothing is more common than
unsuccessful men with talent.
Genius will not; unrewarded genius is
almost a proverb.
Education will not; the world is full
of educated derelicts.
Persistence and determination
are alone supreme."

Calvin Coolidge

"Until one is committed there is hesitancy, the chance to draw back, always ineffectiveness. Concerning all acts of initiative (and creation), there is one elementary truth, the ignorance of which kills countless ideas and splendid plans: that the moment one definitely commits oneself, then Providence moves too.

"All sorts of things occur to help one that would never otherwise have occurred. A whole stream of events issues from the decision, raising in one's favour all manner of unforeseen incidents and meetings and material assistance, which no man could have dreamt would have come his way. I have learned a deep respect for one of Goethe's couplets: 'Whatever you can do, or dream you can, begin it. Boldness has genius, power, and magic in it.' "

W.H. Murray
"The Scottish Himalayan Expedition"

44

Enthusiasm is infectious.
Nobody else will get excited about what
you're doing
unless you do.
Enthusiasm will ignite the fire.
You've got to strike the match.

Spectators are enthusiastic
for the day of the game.
Players are enthusiastic
for days of the season.
Champions are enthusiastic
for all the days of their lives.

It is not possible to always feel confident.
It is absolutely essential to always
exhibit confidence.

Get in the habit of exhibiting confidence.
Something magical will happen.
You will feel confident.

When you feel confident, you have faith.
Faith is action in the face of doubt.

Exhibit confidence in the face of doubt.

Six Rules for Exhibiting Confidence:

1. Smile.
2. Wear the best clothing you can afford.
3. Look everyone straight in the eye.
4. Stand tall.
5. Relax.
6. Speak with strength in your voice.

Chapter Six

Don't Blow It on the Small Stuff

Be prepared.
Do your homework.
Agreement is often won or lost before
the first words have been spoken.

Be prepared
to get people thinking about
the big picture.

Be prepared
to get people thinking about
winning.

Be prepared
to get people thinking about
the unlimited possibilities.

Here is the small stuff you must know.
1) Your personal strengths.
2) Your personal weaknesses.
3) Your organization.
4) Your objective for each encounter.

You should also know the people you are persuading.
1) Their personal strengths.
2) Their personal weaknesses.
3) Their long- and short-term goals.
4) Their personal needs.

Knowledge is power.
Whoever knows more will maintain control.

A great manager is
an expert,
a consultant,
an adviser,
a counselor,
a guide,
a mentor,
a specialist,
a coach,
an ace,
an authority,
an educator,
a champion.

Great managers are not born,
they are dedicated to greatness.

Chapter Seven

How to Sell Yourself Every Time

Try this. Next time you are with an
infant, look into his eyes and smile. In
a soft, loving tone, recite the Pledge of
Allegiance. How does the child react? How
much of its reaction is based on the Pledge
and how much on the way you said it?

The facts are well-documented. Many studies,
including one by Dr. Albert Mehrabian of
the University of Southern California,
conclude that people form opinions and react
to you on the basis of three modalities:
visual, vocal, and verbal.

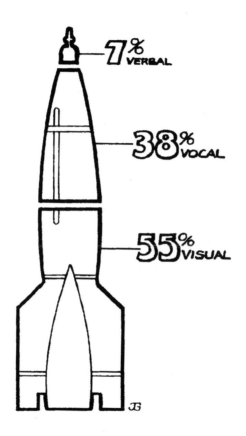

7% VERBAL

38% VOCAL

55% VISUAL

Visual communication is nonverbal—
how you look when you communicate.
Visual communication includes
facial expression, eye contact, clothing,
grooming, gestures, posture, and movement.

Vocal communication is how you sound
when you speak.
Vocal communication includes
volume, expression, clarity, and speed.

Verbal communication is words.

If you improve your
visual, vocal, and verbal
communication skills,
people will believe in you.
You will sell yourself.
You will sell your vision.

Chapter Eight

Selling Your Ideas

Selling your ideas is a process, not an event.
The Close begins when you open.

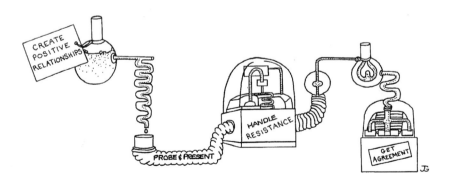

You don't need to know 1,001 tricky ways to manipulate people.

You don't need to manipulate people to persuade them.

Successful persuasion is a natural
by-product of a positive relationship.

Focus on creating
positive relationships.

People are persuaded by people they trust.

Master the art of creating positive relationships.
You'll persuade lots of people.
Master the art of creating positive relationships.
You'll eliminate the unspoken objection:
"I don't trust you."

58

One of my dearest friends is a lady
named Almeida. She came to live in
America from a small country in West
Africa. Almeida is a quiet woman of
few but well-chosen words. She has
a magical, powerful effect on everyone
who meets her.

Once she was my guest at a party.
She spent just a few minutes speaking
with a variety of people. Later, one by
one, I encountered many of the people
who attended the party. Almost always,
the first question they would ask
was, "How is Almeida?"

I asked Almeida, "Why do you have such
a magnetic effect on people?" She
replied, "Paul, it is my belief every
person I meet has something to teach me,
and therefore I treat them with honor
and respect."

There is a sales adage:
"Give something for free."
Some salespeople give pens.
Some give a free 30-day supply.
Others give a free consultation.

It works for salespeople.
It will work for you.

You possess an unlimited supply of
one of life's most priceless treasures.
Money can't buy it.

Everyone wants it.
Everyone needs it.

Give it away.
You'll create lots of positive relationships.
You'll persuade lots of people.

Use the Four C's:
Conversation.
Common ground.
Care.
Compliments.

Conversation based on common ground will show that you care. Don't forget a few sincere compliments.

Chapter Nine

The Answer Is Contained Within the Question

Play Sherlock Holmes.

The three Most Important Persuasion Skills:
Knowing how to ask smart questions.
Knowing how to listen.
Knowing how to present the right answers.

Maintain control at all times.
Give up control, and you give up your goal.
Maintain control with questions.

You might start with,
"Do you mind if I ask you a few questions?"

Then,
"May I take a few notes?"

(The mind is for thinking;
the pen is for remembering.)

Great achievements always
begin with great plans.

Plans are merely road maps.
Many times there are better ways to get there.

Ask questions
to gain involvement for your plan.

Ask questions
to gather new ideas.

Ask questions
to find exactly the right people
to carry out your plan.

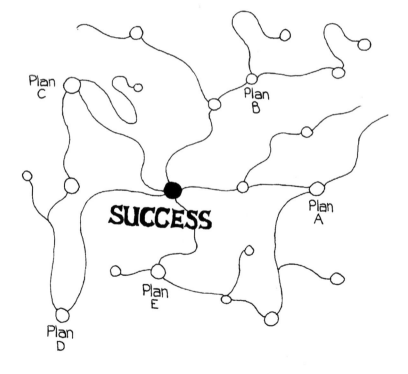

Plan C

Plan B

Plan A

SUCCESS

Plan E

Plan D

70

Ask questions to uncover needs.

What problems can you solve?
What benefits can you provide?

If you discover a difficulty or discomfort,
don't be afraid to "gently touch the hurt."
You will confirm the need to take the
positive action you are prescribing,
and you will discover ways
you can provide solutions.

The road to agreement
is paved with lots of little questions
to which the answers are yes.
Get lots of little yeses.

74

Don't forget the big question:
Ask for what you want.

After you ask,
zip the lip.

You will be amazed at what happens
when you ask.

Chapter Ten

Are You Listening?

Consider this: Your health aside,
your happiness will be determined by your
relationships with other people.
Life without successful relationships is a
shell. Similarly, if your life is
filled with loving connections with
friends and family and with harmonious
associations with colleagues and clients,
you have achieved the greater part of
success.

Your ability to communicate effectively
will dictate the quality of your
relationships.

My mother was born in Czechoslovakia.
In 1939, her parents decided to send her
and her sister on a visit to America.
It was to be the last time she would see
her parents and the rest of her family.
Hitler invaded her country shortly after
she left. My mother loved her new
homeland. She dedicated herself to becoming
a "real" American.

She learned to speak perfect English
with crystal clarity and distinct pride.

She taught me two simple truths:
The first is, "Speak loudly and clearly if
you expect people to listen."
The second is, "Learn to
get along with people."

I have discovered my mother's two simple
admonitions are among life's most profound
challenges. They are inseparable.

I have since learned a corollary to my
mother's teachings: If you want people
to listen, you must first listen to them.

Listening is not simply a courtesy.
It is the most overlooked talent of
all great managers.

Managing is 80% listening and 20% speaking.

Chances are, if you are speaking more than
20% of the time, you're probably
failing in your ability to motivate people.

It is more important for you to become an
interested person
than an interesting person.

The eloquence of your own silence
will pay handsome dividends.

Prepare to listen:
KEEP QUIET.
DON'T TALK.
SHUT UP.

Listen visually:
What do his or her
clothing, grooming, body language, and
eye contact say to you?

Listen vocally:
Unspoken feelings will be revealed
in the sound of his or her voice.

Listen verbally:
What do the words mean?

After listening,
match your visual, vocal, and verbal style
to the person you are speaking with.

You will create instant rapport.
You will create success
in the simple art of persuasion.

People like people like themselves.

Chapter Eleven

How to Deliver a Perfect Presentation

The persuasive manager
identifies needs and concerns
to determine which benefits to present.

The persuasive manager
keeps the discussion
focused on benefits.

Professional salespeople do not sell
products or services.
Professional salespeople sell
benefits.
Learn from them.

Persuasive managers
present only those benefits
that match the needs and concerns
of the people they are persuading.

Just as in sales,
people are persuaded for emotional reasons,
then justify their decisions
with logic.

You must create a presentation
that arouses the emotions.

Your presentation should create
an emotional attachment.

How creative are you?
Employ words that excite the senses.
Have your presentation paint pictures.
Allow the person you are persuading to
see, feel, hear, smell, and touch the
benefits.

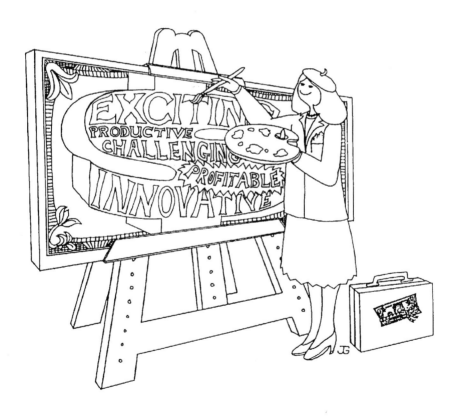

Chapter Twelve

How to Overcome Objections

The only objection you can't handle
is the one you don't hear.
Become an
Objection Hound.

Successful managers know that
objections are defense
mechanisms people use to
resist change.

Sniff out the
objection and you hold
the key to
effective persuasion.

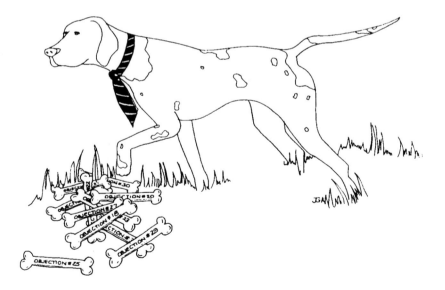

Create rapport.
Create positive relationships.

You will eliminate the prime objection:
Fear.
All other objections are secondary.

You need not fear secondary objections.
They are normal and natural.

They are good signs.
They are requests for more information.
They are details you must negotiate.
You will often hear the same secondary
objections.

The secret to handling them is to memorize
your answers in advance.

Bring them out into the open.
Give them AIR.

Acknowledge all objections.

Never argue.
Show concern and understanding.
Honor the dignity of the people you speak with.

Isolate all objections.

Identify the obstacle.
What are its dimensions?

Respond to each of them.

Secondary objections are questions.
Answer them with benefits.

The two most common objections are:
"We don't have the time"
and
"We've done it before and it didn't work."

Never attempt to argue about them.
Acknowledge and explain.

Sell the benefits.
Sell the value.
Sell the vision.

You will eradicate all resistance.

Chapter Thirteen

Now, Shake the Money Tree

Every time you sell an idea,
you create opportunities.

You create opportunities for yourself to grow.
You create opportunities for your people to grow.

Success starts with enthusiasm for a new idea.
Success is contagious.

Selling the idea is not the end.
It is the beginning.
An accepted idea is a seed.
Watch your business grow.
Watch your career grow.

Create lots of positive relationships.
You'll create a powerful network.

Most career opportunities occur
through networking.

Networking provides you
with valuable information.

Networking is the key
to expanding your influence.

Networking will unlock
your personal power.

Work your net:
Keep your positive relationships alive.

Networking works.
Keep your net working.

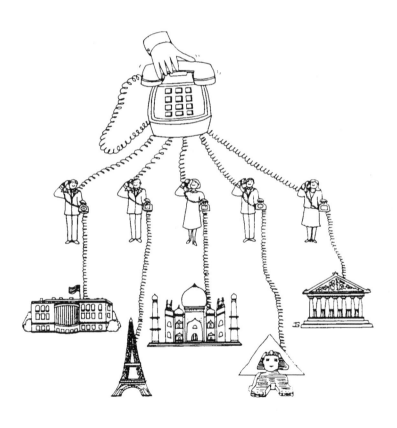

Chapter Fourteen

How to Achieve Your Goals

In college, I secretly admired certain young women and often felt that they were attracted to me. Yet I rarely dated. Many weekends I sat home alone.

In my class there was a young man named Harvey Langston. Harvey was of average intelligence, had no athletic ability, and was not considered handsome. What Harvey had were frequent, attractive dates.

One day out of sheer frustration I asked, "How do you do it?" He replied, "If you ask enough of them enough times…"

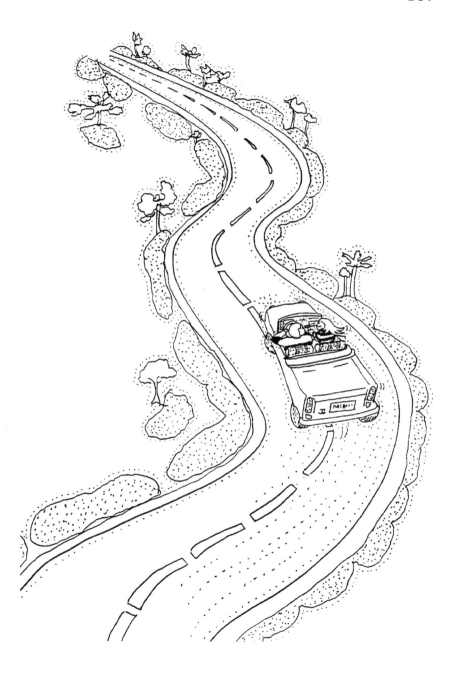

Successful management is a game
of simple mathematics.
If you want to get lots of Yeses,
then you've got to get lots of Noes.

If you present only one idea,
you have only one chance for success.

If you present five ideas,
then you have multiplied
your opportunities for success.

Learn to love Noes.
It takes lots of Noes to get Yes.

(Although success requires failure,
keep it at a minimum.)

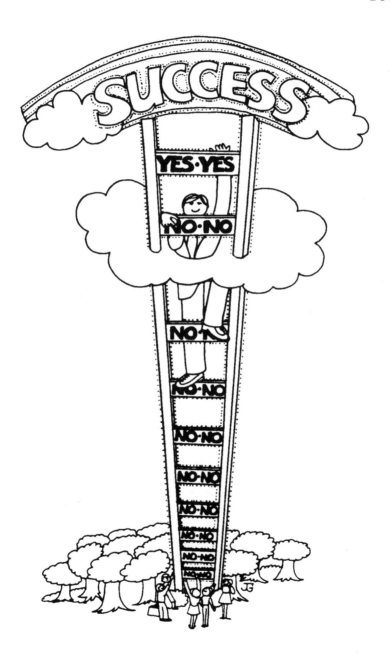

Chapter Fifteen

Making Dreams Come True

FIRST, DREAM.

Treasure your dreams.
They are the product of your heart,
the source of your passion,
the food of your spirit.

If you dream magnificent dreams,
set realistic goals,
and proceed steadily and patiently,
you will experience
the thrill of victory.
Your life will be filled with triumph.

112

THEN VISUALIZE AND AFFIRM YOUR SUCCESS.

Visualizing is a process as old as mankind.

"The greatest discovery of our age has been that we, by changing the inner aspects of our thinking, can change the outer aspects of our lives."

William James

My buddy Bob uses visualizations
and affirmations effectively.
He says,
"There's a cloud over my head."
And there is.
The question is,
Are you aware of what you visualize?
Are you using POSITIVE visualizations and
affirmations?

Be positive.
Visualize your success.
See it, hear it, smell it, feel it.
Draw pictures of it;
make up songs about it.
Experience it.

Imagine that you have already
achieved it.

Be sure to visualize
successful outcomes of your efforts.

Top Ten Management Affirmations:

1. I set realistic, measurable goals.
2. My first goal is to create positive
   relationships.
3. I believe in myself, my organization,
   and the product of my efforts.
4. I take an interest in others, and they
   take an interest in me.
5. I actively listen to all
   visual, vocal, and verbal communication.

6. I am conscious of my visual, vocal, and verbal presentations and continually seek to improve them.
7. I treat all people with respect and dignity.
8. I am not afraid of being told No and understand that failure is a necessary component of my success.
9. I nourish myself physically, mentally, emotionally, and spiritually.
10. I use positive thoughts, affirmations, and visualizations to make my dreams a reality.

ALWAYS BE YOURSELF.

Can you imagine a world with only
one kind of restaurant to choose from?

Or one kind of music?
Or one kind of art?
Or one kind of automobile?
Or one kind of management style?

You are unique.

Celebrate your uniqueness.
Emulate, don't imitate.
Identify the ingredients of greatness.

Create your own recipe.

Before you know it,
people will try to imitate you.
That's quite a compliment.
(But they'll never be great until they
create their own recipe.)

Chapter Sixteen

My Wish for You

I wish for you peace of mind,
    because joy abides here.
I wish for you a healthy body, for without it
    it is impossible to enjoy
    even the most simple pleasures of life.
I wish for you to be gentle and loving to
    yourself; celebrate your strengths, and
    be patient with yourself in areas in which you
    are growing and learning.
I wish for you to trust your inner voice;
    this is the source of your wisdom.
    It is never wrong.
I wish for you to make the child within you
    your best friend; counsel that child
    when it is frightened; let it out to play
    when it is safe; and always love it
    unconditionally.
I wish for you to treasure your sense of
    humor; your ability to laugh and smile
    is one of the true measures of your
    success in living.

I wish for you to invest your time and energy
 in your relationships; these are the
 sparkling jewels of your life.
I wish for you to continue to open your heart;
 this above all else will make this world
 a better place to live.
There is a song within you
 full of hope and joy and peace
 and love.
It is a song only you can sing.
I wish for you to sing your song;
 sing it out,
 and all the world will sing along.

Epilogue

Curiosity breeds aliveness.
Openness allows for unlimited possibilities.
Creativity is natural for the receptive mind.

Maintain an attitude of being reachable.
Invest in your education.
Your success is unlimited.

Great minds know what they don't know.

"To laugh is to risk appearing the fool.
To weep is to risk appearing sentimental.
To reach out to another
      is to risk involvement.
To expose your feelings
      is to risk exposing yourself.
To place your ideas and your dreams
      before the crowd is to risk ridicule.
But risks must be taken, because the greatest
      risk in life is to risk nothing.
The person who risks nothing, does nothing,
      has nothing, and is nothing.
He may avoid suffering and sorrow,
      but he simply cannot learn to feel
      —or to grow
      —or to love
      —or to live.
Chained by his certitudes, he is a slave.
Only the person who risks is truly free."

Anonymous

About the author

Paul Karasik is one of America's leading business consultants and lecturers. His list of Fortune 500 clients is a Who's Who of American business. An award-winning salesman who speaks from 18 years of personal experience, Karasik is president of The Business Institute, a sales and management training company that annually trains thousands of men and women. He is also president of the American Seminar Leaders Association and author of two books, *Sweet Persuasion: The Illustrated Guide to Closing the Sale* (Simon & Schuster) and *How to Make It Big in the Seminar Business* (McGraw-Hill).

Products and services offered by Paul Karasik:

- Keynote Speeches
- Motivational Programs
- Sales Training
- Audio and Video Learning Systems
- Customized Sales and Management Training

For more information on how Paul Karasik can increase your professional success, please call or write:

The Business Institute
899 Boulevard East, Suite 6A
Weehawken, New Jersey 07087

Phone (201) 864-9149 or Toll-Free (800) 735-0511